Future

Passages

Central Pennsylvania
Icons Your
Children
May Never
Know

Robert M. Kurtz Jr.

Historic
Regional Photographs
of Central Pennsylvania

Second printing, December 1998

Library of Congress Catalog Number: 98-96360

ISBN 0-9665451-0-9

Published by Robert M. Kurtz, Jr., Clearfield, Pennsylvania

Designed by Murphy Communications, State College, Pennsylvania

Printed by Jostens Commercial Printing Services, State College, Pennsylvania

Printed in the USA

To Marilyn

*without whose love and understanding
this book would not have
been completed.*

Preface

In this book of photographs I present a pictorial perspective on central Pennsylvania, particularly Clearfield and Clearfield County, in the 1990s. My hope is to preserve this area's historical sites and landmarks, past and present, through photography. Compiling this pictorial document has less to do with recording the present than with how the present will someday look as the past.

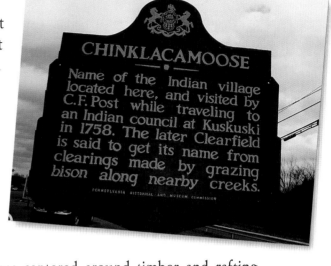

These photographs are not historic in the sense that important events happened where they were taken, but historic in the sense that they record a period of time. My intention has been to photograph a way of life and a landscape that are changing—changing out of existence as all things and people do, yet I seek to preserve them for the future through photographs.

The central geographic region for this book is the town of Clearfield, whose name comes from the cleared fields where bison used to roam. The town was known to the Indians as Chinklacamoose, and as Clearfield Town or Old Town to the early settlers. Its history has centered around timber and rafting, lumber, farming, clay, stone, and later coal. In addition to Clearfield, other neighboring towns and counties in central Pennsylvania are included as well.

These photographs are not meant to simply be pretty pictures, but to present an historical document of the 1990s. Like Walker Evans (we're both alumni of The Mercersburg Academy), who photographed in the 1930s, I attempt to record common scenes often taken for granted.

Many of these photographs highlight local scenes that will someday vanish. I've photographed barns that disappeared a week later (due to fire), and I've lost some chances to get wonderful pictures because I felt that I could always go back. To my regret they were not there later. A few years from now there will be even fewer Mail Pouch barns. They will have gone the way of the Burma-Shave signs, none of which are to be seen today. They remain only as pictures in the minds of some of us, and will disappear when we do.

A few of the pictures in this book have family significance, but I have tried to limit that; of those that do, I've included early settlers and their pioneering role in the region. The scope of some of these was greater than expected as I discovered historic facts which added other dimensions to the photographs. One small obscure country cemetery yielded

far more information on early settlers, family and nonfamily, than I could have ever anticipated. Many such cemeteries provide interesting insights and historic information if one knows where and how to look, and what questions to ask.

With this type of document, there is always another picture to be taken, there is always another idea or subject that should have been included but wasn't. At some point, however, I must stop photographing and publish. There isn't room in one book, or time for one photographer, to record all the scenes that deserve to be included. As with all writers and photographers, I've included photographs and information on subjects of particular interest to me. Others would include different subjects. I hope that this book encourages others to compile similar types of historical and pictorial documents. The possibilities for photography of this type are unlimited; any geographic region provides boundless opportunities.

Because I know the joy and frustration of tracking down specific historic sites written about or photographed in other books, I frequently include some basic location data so that an interested person can find many of the places I've photographed, with a reasonable degree of success. Following Civil War troop movements in the Shenandoah Valley and Oregon Trail wagon ruts as they crossed the continent, or seeking the old military post of Ojo Caliente on the Apache Reservation in New Mexico, has given me a feel for the value of such information. My pictures from these explorations, and others, must await a future volume, however.

Unless otherwise identified, most photographs were taken in Clearfield or the immediate vicinity. Nature and wildlife photographs were taken in my backyard.

I hope all who look at this book enjoy it and learn something of interest.

Robert M. Kurtz Jr.

Clearfield, Pennsylvania
March 28, 1998

Time eats all things.
The brown gold of autumn says so.
The falling leaves in the last rainwind before
the first spit of snow—they have their way of saying,
Listen, be quiet, winter comes:
Time eats all things.

Carl Sandburg
Remembrance Rock

To Deb & J.C.!
Best Wishes!
Enjoy.
Bob Kurtz

Robert M. Kurtz Jr.

214 Charles Road
Clearfield, PA 16830

Natural,
Historic &
Architectural
Imagery

Photoessayist

Debbie —

Here is a copy of my book which
will give you and J.C. an idea of
what I photograph.

It was nice talking with you.
I'll be in touch again shortly to
plan the October 10 - Sunday photo
tour with you.

My best,
Bob Kurtz

7/28/99

(814) 765 - 6561 daytime

A Personal Perspective of History

Since in this book the 1990s are presented in an historical context, it seems appropriate to look at my personal interpretation and understanding of what is history.

History, in my opinion, is the portrayal of events taken in the context of the times as seen through the eyes of people who lived in those times.

All history becomes obscure through the passage of time. We seldom can visualize the reality of people living, thinking, and dealing with events at any particular moment in time. Most history is played out against the backdrop of ordinary events and people who often exert far more influence, particularly in a democratic society, than they are given credit for.

Photographs record the real world. They do not lend themselves to change in the way that historical writings, through the author's interpretation or opinions, often do.

History is *not* the portrayal of events tempered by hindsight. Such an approach often changes history, and although at best is unintentional, at its worst it rewrites history for "political correctness." For example, the elimination of photographs and remembrances of Franklin Roosevelt with his trademark cigarette and holder or Eleanor Roosevelt in her fox fur neckpiece is considered by some to be politically correct history. Not that the appearance of these items changes history, but they were so much a part of that period and President and Mrs. Roosevelt that to alter, change, or obliterate such things, in my opinion, corrupts history.

Often we view past events in today's light, not seeing the thought pattern of the time in which they occurred, but rather through the prism of current thought, looking back with the advantage of hindsight not available to those living at the time the events occurred. We seldom recognize a period until it has gone by. Until it lies behind us it is merely everyday life.

I wish to present history lived—or in this case, looked at—and recorded as seen, interpreted, and understood *now*, not with the perspectives which go with hindsight, and so often alter history relatively quickly after it is lived. Every minute, every hour, adds to history and changes how events are remembered. Historians, at least in the details, often guess at what actually happened.

Marcel Proust once said that when he came to die he would take all his great men with him, since they could never be at all the same to anyone else. And so it is with us. We, too, shall take our great men in the sense of our time, material environment, and those we know with us. The visions of life and those events and people we know can never be at all the same to anyone else. The best we can do is try to capture through photographs or writing the things we know. And so, what is here today will be gone tomorrow.

If my perceptions of the 1990s are correct, the world is now embarking upon an era of unprecedented economic, medical, and technological development that will fascinate historians and archaeologists much as the continental movement westward or the Civil War fascinate us. Those historians will look on this time, wishing they could revisit this era just as Civil War reenactors do today, or much as many would give their eyeteeth to have been present, even for a short while, in Philadelphia during the hot, humid summer of 1787 as the Constitutional Convention was meeting, or in the 1860s, only a short 130-odd years ago, when any citizen had access to President Lincoln.

Only a few decades from now it will be difficult to imagine that today we still remember veterans of World War I (yes, a few) and World War II. Many of us recall living at a time when Winston Churchill was Prime Minister of England, or Dwight Eisenhower was President, or Joe DiMaggio played for the New York Yankees, or man first walked on the moon. No matter how humdrum or unimportant life may seem to us living today, we will someday be looked at with great fascination.

In this book I seek to capture what is here today, but may soon pass from the scene. In a few years what you see here will exist only in memories; after that, it will vanish like a dream, yet it will still hold fascination as one of the great turning points of history. What wouldn't they give, those men and women of centuries to come, to be able to witness firsthand not just the great public events of our time but simply what it was like to be alive as the twentieth century drew to a close.

Obscure Destinies is the title Willa Cather gave to a collection of three of her most memorable short stories. The title, of course, was suggested by Thomas Gray in his famous "Elegy." As in these stories, obscure destinies, brought on by the passage of time, await us all, but that does not in any way detract from the importance of each individual life or the influence we have at any particular time.

We tend to look at history only through events that have taken place, rather than, in Winston Churchill's phrase, through the emotions of "blood, toil, tears and sweat" experienced by people who live during any particular time. Churchill's phrase, while used in a different context, still sums up in those four simple words nearly all events of history. A liberal translation, yes, but an appropriate one.

Much of history can be written as the story of man seeking freedom from either oppression or drudgery. Freedom from oppression comes from democracy and elimination of prejudice; freedom from drudgery, through inventions and technology. Both change as society moves on. The writings and speeches of Thomas Jefferson, and even of Abraham Lincoln, had a different meaning, taken in the context of their time, as opposed to the interpretations given them today. It is incredible to realize that Jefferson gave but two public speeches during his eight years as president. What a difference between then and now.

Great individuals make for great nations and less great individuals make for less great nations—or at least nations not quite so great. Character in individuals translates into the character of nations.

Much of the value of history is in understanding what has gone before and, through that, why we are where we are today. To properly understand history, it becomes necessary to look at why things were done and written as they were at a particular time, rather than to criticize individuals for what they did. Not all history is pleasant to read. Much of it may even be repulsive, but to deprive anyone of the best writings of history and literature, or to change them, because they might offend a particular group, is to deprive us of our heritage.

The French historian Jules Michelet wisely wrote, "The end is nothing, the road is all." And so it is as we move through our time in history making our own separate and individual contribution, which, when combined with the contributions of millions of others, writes the history of this time. And just as we are a product of all we have read and seen, certainly of all we have been taught, so society, which shapes us, has been shaped itself by all that has gone before.

The people we know today, and those who know us, will someday have passed into the mists of time. Those graves we now tend will become untended, just as our graves will be untended by today's tenders, until any memories of us, or this time in history, have passed into oblivion. Few will even venture to guess what it was like to have been alive in the 1990s, all those many years ago. Because of this rich and varied past, however, we have great hope and expectations for the future.

Historic
Regional Photographs
of Central Pennsylvania

Slant House

Near Knobs Fire Tower.

Centre Furnace

Erected in 1792 by Colonels John Patton and Samuel Miles,
officers in the American Revolutionary War.
Its product, the first iron melted in Centre County,
was carried on mule-back to Pittsburgh.
This industry played an important role in the development of State College
and the establishment of the Farmers High School (later Penn State).
The old Bellefonte Pike can be seen in the background.
Located on the Benner Pike, Route 26, northeast of State College,
adjacent to the Centre Furnace Mansion.

Cigar Factory

Route 522, Main Street, Shirleysburg.
Built about 1850 as a blacksmith shop, it later became a cigar
factory. The tobacco came from Lancaster County.

Kratzer House

Located at 104 East Cherry Street, Clearfield,
this house was built in 1842, making it the town's oldest home.
In Greek Revival style, it has corner columns, eyebrow windows,
and board and batten siding.

Thomas Holt and Jennie Reighard Murray Home

120 South Second Street.
Mr. Murray was a distinguished lawyer, churchman,
and public speaker in the late 1800s and early 1900s.
He published three volumes, each titled *Speeches*.
He also organized and was the first president of the Clearfield County Historical Society.
The home, built in 1880, is of Italianate design
with Tudor-style dripstones on the windows and quoins at the corners.
The cupola is surrounded by distinctive chimneys.

Yeaney House

111 South Second Street.
Built in 1887.
Demolished in 1996 for a parking lot.

Historical Society

104 East Pine Street.
Built in 1879, this and the Murray House are the only
two remaining houses in Clearfield with a cupola.

Red, White, and Blue
Barber Pole and Shop

Shoe Repair Shop

209 West Nichols Street.
Mr. Sorbera has been in the shoe repair business since 1935.
He has the last of eight such shops in Clearfield.

Goldenrod and Bee

Autumn Foliage

Lower Witmer Park

Both Lower and Upper Witmer Parks were given
to the Borough of Clearfield by Abraham Witmer in 1805.
In addition, he gave land for the courthouse,
jail, a market, and an academy.

Presbyterian Church
Built in 1867-1869.

1831 Book of Psalms and Hymns
Ebenezer Betts, 1766-1846.
Currently in a personal collection.

Presbyterian Church Garden

Dedicated in 1993 to Rev. Frederick Gregory Betts,
Pastor from 1840 to 1844, and his descendants.
Rev. Betts served the congregations at Curwensville (Pike Township)
and Fruit Hill while minister in Clearfield.
He preached in barns, schoolhouses, homes,
and at crossroad settlements throughout the county.
In three years, he gave 405 sermons and covered 6,444
miles on horseback or wagon.
On December 17, 1843, he preached a sermon on temperance
that was so well received it was published in its entirety,
covering the entire front and most of the back page of the February 28, 1844,
issue of the Clearfield weekly newspaper, *The Democratic Banner.*

Man was lost and saved in a garden.
Blaise Pascal

Girard Township Grange Hall

The Grange is a social and political organization
comprised mainly of rural and farm families.
This Grange Hall was built prior to 1897.

Stone Structure

Route 96, Bedford County.

Farmer's Market

Belleville.

Amish Washday

Buggy Parking, Farmer's Market

Belleville.

Amish on Bus Tour

Outdoor Cigarette Advertising

End of an era?

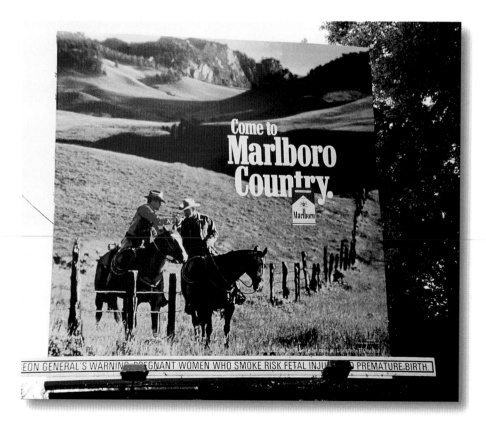

Mail Pouch Barn

Juncture of Routes 219 and 286.

Barn Near Eagles Mere

Sullivan County.

Barn Door

Country Road Guardrail

Simple guardrails seldom seen today
except on rural country roads.

1821 Mile Marker
Philadelphia-Erie Turnpike

Off Route 879 near Curwensville on the road to Glen Richey.
Many Indian paths converged in the Chinklacamoose
(Clearfield) area. Among them were Bald Eagle's Path,
Kittanning Path, Warriors Mark Path, Great Shamokin Path,
Mead's Path, Frankstown Path, Raystown-Chinklacamoose Path,
and Venango-Chinklacamoose Path.
Today, these paths, which frequently followed streams
through valleys and across hills,
often have roads built over or near them.

24

Harvest Time in a Corn Field

Rockville Bridge across the Susquehanna River

Route 322, north of Harrisburg.
Built in 1902, this forty-eight-span bridge is the longest
stone arch railroad bridge in the world.
Much of the stone came from Curwensville stone quarries.

R. Dudley Tonkin
Raftman's Memorial Timber Dam in Winter

Built in 1974, this wooden dam
(strongly reinforced with concrete for permanency)
is reminiscent of the old splash dams built during rafting days
to hold water and logs prior to releasing them downstream.
The timber brand used to mark logs shown below is that of Weaver & Betts.

Ŧ, W + B

Stone Canal Works along the Juniata River

Routes 22 and 322, located 1.7 miles east of Lewistown.
This was built in the early 1830s as part of
an extensive canal system in central Pennsylvania.

Indian Mill

Route 322 east of Clearfield.
The depression in the center of this large stone was used
by the Indians for grinding their corn and maize.
The stone is located near the convergence of several Indian paths.

Old Stone Farmhouse

Along Route 75.

Log House

Off Route 322 north of Lewistown.

Abandoned Railroad Bridge

Rails to Trails, a system of turning abandoned railroad beds into hiking trails,
has transformed this bridge crossing the West Branch of the Susquehanna River.

McGees Mills Covered Bridge

Built in 1873, this is the last covered bridge over
the West Branch of the Susquehanna River.
Its design, a 122-foot arch-truss span, was patented in 1804.
This photo was taken before its reconstruction
after the winter storm of 1993.

Unpainted Classic-Style Farmhouse

Barnyard, Barn, and Horses

Along Route 286.

Schoolhouse, Church, Community Center,
Grange, and Election Hall

Goshen Township.

Pinchot Road

Narrow Pennsylvania roads of the 1920s and 1930s,
so named for Republican Governor Gifford Pinchot (1923-1927 and 1931-1935),
who had them built to fulfill his campaign promise "to get the farmer out of the mud."
Pinchot was an early conservationist, twice Governor,
when consecutive terms were not permitted.
(facing page)

Dead Corn, End of the Season

Octagonal Barn

This unpainted barn was built between 1860 and 1880.
Not only is it unique by virtue of having eight sides, it also has a slate roof.
Located in Jefferson County, it can be found off Route 28 (going south from Brookville).
At the town of Sommerville, turn left on SR 3007 toward Heathville.
Just south of town, turn left on SR 3022 and go through the Carrier Cemetery.
The barn is less than a mile farther, in Clover Township.

Round Barn

Route 45, near Old Fort, Centre County.
Built in 1910.

Fall Harvest

Hay rolls secured in protective white plastic.

Barn and Barnyard Gate

Woolridge Farm.

Mail Pouch Barn with Crown Vetch

Route 28 south of Brookville.

Country Barn

This barn, near Woodland, collapsed
several years ago due to age.

Snake in Lilac Tree

Raccoon Climbing Tree

Backyard Bear

Photo by Marilyn.

Raccoon Mother and Cubs

Frozen Tree

On a frosty fall morning.

Spring Redbud in Bloom

Route 16, near Mercersburg.

Dogwood, the Beginnings of Spring

Route 322, east of Philipsburg.

Bicentennial Oak Tree and Mount Nittany

Between 102 and 104 Farmstead Lane, State College.
This tree has been jointly recognized by the
National Arborist Association and the International Society of Arboriculture
as being on this site in 1787,
the year of the Constitution's adoption.

Murray Cemetery

On April 7, 1821, John and Mary Murray arrived from Shaver's Creek Valley, Huntingdon County,
to the Lecontes Mills area in Clearfield County, a distance of nearly 60 miles.
They were the fourth family in the township. After John's death less than three years later, in January 1824,
Mary was left with seven young children, the oldest thirteen. She refused to separate the family,
insisting that they could survive in the wilderness. However, with no money and no goods to trade,
the family was desperate to get through the early summer of 1825 until the crops came in.
Mary's only choice was to send her son Alexander to his grandfather William Ewing's farm
back in the Shaver's Creek Valley, to borrow five dollars to purchase the needed goods.
In June 1825, Alexander, aged twelve, made the 120-mile round trip through the woods and forest alone
with only the flintlock gun that had been his father's and the family dog accompanying him.
On his return, a mile from home, he shot a bear, which provided much-needed food for the family.

Murray Cemetery

Lecontes Mills, Girard Township.

Isabella Meek Holt Murray, 1820-1879
Alexander Murray, 1812-1889
John Murray, 1785 or 1786-1824
Mary Anderson Ewing Murray, 1790-1871

Elmer Ellsworth Murray

An interesting historical note
is the name of this child,
who lived 1 year, 3 months, and 13 days.
Elmer Ellsworth was a colonel in the Union
Army, had been a close friend of Lincoln and
the Lincoln family, and was perhaps the first
Union fatality of the Civil War.
He became a legend after being shot on
May 24, 1861, taking down the flag of secession
from the Marshall House, a second-class hotel in
Alexandria, Virginia.
Ellsworth was so close to Lincoln that his death
brought Lincoln to tears.
His body lay in state in the White House.
This child was born August 31, 1861. One
wonders how many young boys received the
names of heroes due to their parents' feelings
for the Union or Confederate cause.

Gravestone Detail

Many gravestones, particularly these from
the 1800s, made use of stone carvings and
etchings. Much of this art has been lost today. In
addition to Bible verses, many stones
listed the person's age in years, months,
and days, and date of death,
but not always date of birth.
Stones were commonly taller
than those used today.
A lamb or dove often was put
on the headstones of children,
while the Tree of Life was frequently
found on adult gravestones.

William Murray

During the journey from Huntingdon County
to Clearfield County in April 1821,
the Murray party unexpectedly encountered
a heavy spring snowstorm.
William, an infant less than two months old,
developed a serious illness that his mother thought
would result in his death and burial along the way.
However, he survived and lived a full life, as attested to
by the information on his gravestone.

Every Day Is Flag Day

Clearfield Post Office.

County Courthouse

Clearfield.
Built in 1860-1862
of Italianate Villa style.

Voting Booth and State Flag

Goldenrod Precinct, Lawrence Township,
Clearfield County.

County Jail

North Front and Second Streets.
Built in 1870-1872.
Used as the Clearfield County Jail until 1981.
Flood high-water marks as shown on the front of the jail:
June 1, 1889—49 inches
March 18, 1936—71 inches

1940 Plymouth Police Car

Bell's Drug Store

This site in Coalport has been a drugstore since 1884.
It has one of the last original soda fountains.

Coalport Hardware Store

A mine supply and hardware store built in 1875.
This store is now in the fourth generation of the McNulty family.
It was established by the Holden family who sold it
to the McNultys before moving to Clearfield at the turn of the century
where they opened the Holden Paint and Hardware Store
at 123 East Market Street.

House at Hegarty's Crossroads

Clearfield County.
Built in 1873, this house has twenty-four rooms,
each with a fireplace, and one secret room.

William and Jane Patton Irvin Home

240 State Street, Curwensville.
Legend has it that the house was built about 1862
by William and Jane Patton Irvin after
campfires from Union troops accidentally burned their other home.
However, another story dates the home between 1835 and 1840.
An Indian burial ground and spring are located nearby.
Jane, mother of fifteen children, was active during the Civil War
in the exchange of captured Union and Confederate troops.
In this effort she and her husband met with President Lincoln and urged his support,
thus gaining the release of her son Colonel E. A. Irvin of the famous Bucktail Regiment.
Three times she passed through Union lines in this endeavor.
She visited hospitals at the battlefields of South Mountain and Antietam.
William was deeply involved throughout his life in the Curwensville business community.
Both supported civic and charitable causes.

Abandoned Fall Road

At the juncture of Routes 969 and 729.

Abandoned Farmhouse

Kirk Gristmill

Grain was processed in this gristmill for
animal and human consumption.
Located in Rockton, it is one of the last of the old mills.
Built in 1885, it was designed so that the space in front
provided adequate height for horse-drawn
wagons to load and unload.
Although located near Anderson Creek,
this mill was steam-powered.

Remains of Stone Gristmill

One mile south of Orbisonia on Route 522.
This mill, along Black Log Creek in Huntingdon County,
burned in 1879.

Civil War Era Barn Interior

Civil War Era Barn

Route 96, Bedford County.
Built in the 1860s during the Civil War.

Super 322 Drive-In Movie Theater

Route 322, east of Clearfield.

Red Rabbit Drive-In

Route 322 at Amity Hall.
Complete with carhops (to serve you in your car)
and Bunnyburgers.

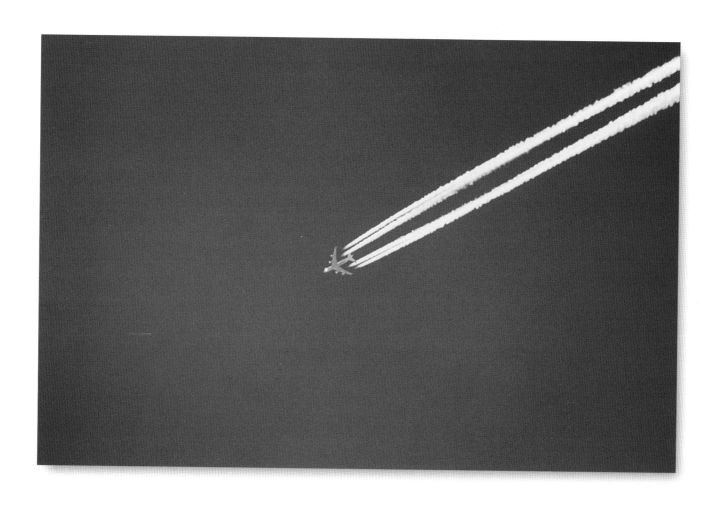

Contrail

Condensation trail from a jet airliner.

Sign at Burnt Cabins

Route 522.
Named for the burning of early settlers' cabins in 1750 to satisfy
Indian protests against white settlers on Indian lands.
The name signifies troubled days on the Pennsylvania frontier.

Tractor Tire Flower Gardens

October Pumpkin Market

Halloween pumpkins, gourds,
and Indian corn for autumn sale.

Milk Can Mailbox

Barn with Brick Silo

Near Curwensville.
Although not all barns have silos,
those that do use them for storage of livestock feed
known as silage.
(facing page)

Orvis Woolridge Barn and Horse

Demolished in 1992 for Wal-Mart distribution center.

Cuppett's Covered Bridge

Route 96, near New Paris, Bedford County.
Built in 1882, this Burr truss bridge is held in place
by a complex set of trusses that interact with an arch that spans
the entire length of the bridge.

Farm Tractor

The annual Antique Farm Equipment Show is held each fall
near Centre Hall in Centre County.

Farm Shed with Tractor

Woolridge farm building, demolished in 1992.

Interior View of an Outhouse

Seating capacity: 2.

Outhouse

Located behind Girard Township Grange Hall.
(facing page)

Barn Interior

Route 522 near Knobsville.

*Barn Construction
and Door Hinge*

Skunk

Fall Backyard

Birch Trees

Elk County.
Marion Brooks State Forest natural area.
(following pages)

Presbyterian Church
Shaver's Creek Manor at Manor Hill

Huntingdon County.
Shaver's Creek Valley, Route 305.
Built in 1823.

Funeral Doors, Manor Hill Church

The double doors at both ends of the church cross-aisle are far above
the ground and have no steps below them.
Reportedly, they are funeral doors,
designed so that wagons bearing coffins could be backed up
to the door at the end of the church next to the road.
The casket was then unloaded into the aisle where, after the funeral service,
it was moved through these doors onto the shoulders of the waiting pallbearers,
who carried it to the cemetery grave site.
It was said that no living person should ever pass through funeral doors.
(facing page)

Country Cemetery, Manor Hill Church

In 1781 or 1782, Katherine (Katie) Ewing,
aged twelve, daughter of Thomas and Mary Reed Ewing
(sister to William Ewing,
whose daughter married John Murray),
and her companion, Betsy McCormick, were kidnapped
by the Indians while berrypicking near their home
in the Shaver's Creek Valley of Huntingdon County.
Taken to Lake Erie, they were separated.
Katie returned to Huntingdon County three years later
by way of Montreal and Philadelphia.
Betsy was later located in Canada by her father,
Alexander McCormick, Sr., who ransomed her
from the Indians.
She later married Katie's brother John.

Elizabeth Anderson Ewing, 1768-1857
William Ewing, 1765-1847

I have been young,
and now am old;

yet have I not
seen the righteous forsaken,

nor his seed
begging bread.

Mary Ewing Murray.
Born in this valley 1790 - Married John
Murray 1807 - Died Clearfield County 1871.

Stained-Glass Window, Manor Hill Church

Given by Thomas H. Murray in memory of
his grandmother Mary Ewing Murray (1790-1871),
an early pioneer who moved to
Clearfield County from Huntingdon County in 1821.

Tree of Life Gravestone Carving

Ring Rock

Located at Miller's Landing where Moshannon Creek joins the West Branch
of the Susquehanna River, above the "Karthaus straight water,"
the ring was placed in a rock as a means of anchoring rafts.
Between 1840 and 1890, the logging and timber industry
employed over 30,000 men and had as many as 2,000 rafts on the river
each spring, providing as much as 300 million board feet of logs a year.
The "Last Raft" went down the river in March, 1938.
Ring Rock can be found by going south on Route 879,
taking the dirt road to the right, just before crossing the bridge at Karthaus.
The road runs parallel to the river about 3.5 miles and ends at the rock.

Stone Marker at the Site of the First
Clearfield County Post Office

Reedsboro, outside of Clearfield
on the road to Glen Richey.
Post office established in 1813.

East Broadtop Railroad

The only narrow-gauge railroad
east of the Mississippi River.
Located in Orbisonia, this railroad has
been in operation since 1873.

Monroe Iron Furnace

Built in 1847 and located near Shaver's Creek Environmental Center,
Route 26, six miles northwest of McAlevy's Fort
at the intersection with Charter Oak Road.
Between 1790 and 1850, many iron furnaces and forges were
located along streams in central Pennsylvania.
They produced Juniata iron, which at that time was the best iron in America.

1888 Mile Marker

Philipsburg Town Square.

Philipsburg Town Hall

Built in 1887.
Decorated for the 1797-1997 Bicentennial.

Madisonburg Post Office

Coalport Central Hotel

Of all the small towns throughout central Pennsylvania,
Coalport has one of the best historic business districts
that give a glimpse into the past.
This hotel, built in 1890, is still in operation today.

5 & 10 Cent Store

One of the last of the five-and-dime stores,
which replaced the older general stores,
is on Main Street, Coalport.
Formerly a Newberry's 5 & 10.

Glen Hope Inn

Built about 1840, this inn,
once known as the Washington House,
was for many years a stagecoach stop
on the Clearfield-Tyrone Turnpike.

Murray Building

19-21 South Second Street.
Built in 1869, reconstructed in 1902.
Law office of Thomas H. Murray
and former county judge Cyrus Gordon.
Now a part of the CNB bank building.

Drainpipes and Downspouts

These drainpipes and downspouts in Mercersburg
which carry rainwater over sidewalks are typical of
roof drainage in many small towns
of south-central Pennsylvania.

Patriotic Flag House

Clearfield County.

Clintonia

Named for American statesman DeWitt Clinton,
a rare, but not endangered, species.

Male Cecropia Moth

Barn and Buttercups

Route 28.

Thacik Rhododendron Gardens

Curwensville.

Mushrooms

Old Doney Farm, Goldenrod area.

Springtime at Walker Gardens

Bigler.
Most extensive gardens between Pittsburgh and Hershey.

West Branch of the Susquehanna River

Juncture of Routes 969 and 729 above
the Curwensville Dam.
(facing page)

Homecoming
Weekend-
The Mercersburg
Academy

Before the Score

Mercersburg 27
Western Reserve 26

Sycamore Lane

The Mercersburg Academy.

The fortune of our lives and our government
depends not exclusively on useful knowledge
but on our character as citizens,
and to form this character
by cultivating the whole man
is the aim of education in the proper sense.

Frederick Augustus Rauch,
First President of Marshall College, 1836-1841
(now The Mercersburg Academy).

Main Hall

The Mercersburg Academy Chapel

Via Crucis Via Lucis
"The Way of the Cross Is the Way of Light."

Buchanan Cabin

This cabin, now located on the Mercersburg Academy campus,
was the birthplace of James Buchanan (1791-1868), 15th President of the United States (1857-1861).
At that time, the cabin was about four miles outside Mercersburg near Cove Gap.

Farmhouse

Abandoned Well

Old Doney Farm, Goldenrod area.

Shirey Barn, Pleasant Valley

Along Route 970. Built in the 1860s.

Chickens, Ducks, and Amish Wash

Barn Shed

Note star painted on this farm shed built in 1855.
Adjacent to Shirey barn.

36 Rural Delivery Mailboxes and 3 Newspaper Boxes

Route 322, near Poe Valley State Park.

Knobs Fire Tower

This sixty-foot-high fire tower,
listed on the National Historic Lookout Register,
was constructed in 1921.
Foresters keep watch over woodlands
during the prime fire danger time
from mid-March through late May,
when the lack of overhead green leaves
causes the bright sun and wind to quickly dry
the brittle leaves and grasses on the forest floor.

Amish Buggy and Corn

Near Barrville.

Amish Farmer

Amish Banking at the Drive-Up Window

Amish Buggies on a Sunday Morning

Amish Milk Cans

Near Barrville.

Women at the Farmer's Market

Belleville.

Amish Wagon and Horse, Farmer's Market
Belleville.

Amish Harvest

Field of bundled or "shocked" oats
placed in circular stacks with a "hudder" on top
to protect them against the weather.

Little League Baseball

Kurtz Field.
Baseball has been played in Clearfield since 1948,
1998 being the 50th year.

Steel Railroad Bridge

Route 28, south of Brookville.

Fishing on the West Branch of the Susquehanna River

Veterans of Foreign Wars Post

These and American Legion Posts, along with Grange and Volunteer Fire Halls,
Elks, Moose, Eagles, Knights of Columbus, and Masonic Lodges and even the
International Order of Odd Fellows (IOOF), as well as the service clubs of Kiwanis,
Rotary, and Lions, are some of the many fraternal organizations
that provide social and charitable needs to local communities.

Roadhouses and Saloons

Also known as bars, pubs, taverns, restaurants, and beer gardens,
they serve as centers of social activity, local hangouts, and gathering spots.

Pine Forest, Winter

Philipsburg Santa

Cutting Your Own Tree at a Christmas Tree Farm

Centre County.

Fungus

Camp TeBoJa, Goshen Township.

Mushrooms

Camp TeBoJa, Goshen Township.

Raccoons and Skunk

Doe and Fawn

White Oak, Union Church Cemetery

According to a ring count by the Penn State School of Forestry,
this tree was estimated to be 351 years old in 1998.
If so, it would have been growing here in 1647.

Philipsburg Union Church

Known as the "Mud Church,"
it was first built of logs, then remodeled in 1842
over the logs to its present form.
It is an outstanding example of simplified
American Gothic architecture.
It also was used as a school.

Egg Hill Church, Autumn

Off Route 45, near Spring Mills, Centre County.
Built in 1860 on a foundation dating to 1838.
Regular use was discontinued in 1927.
Those of the Evangelical faith worshipped here.

Egg Hill Church

Philipsburg Union Church, II

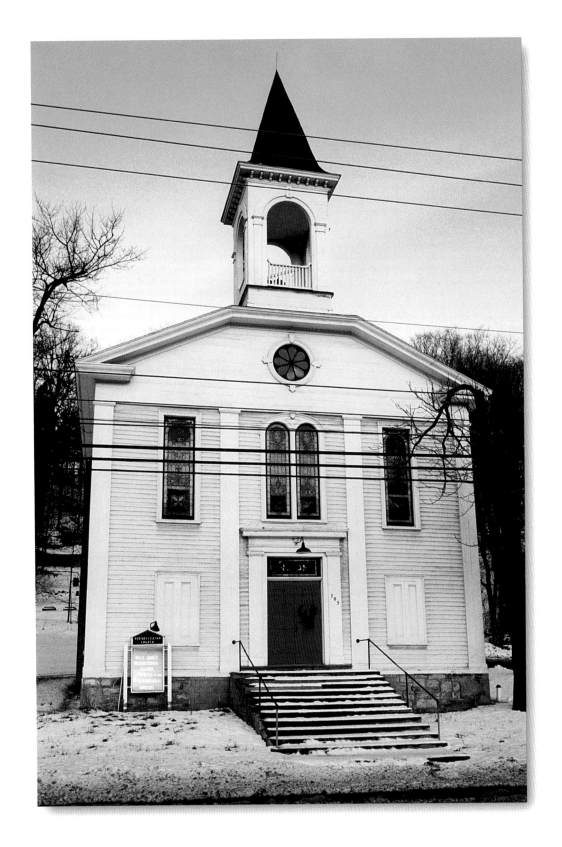

Bald Eagle Presbyterian Church

Located in Port Matilda, this church was built in 1860.

July Fourth Fireworks

State College.

Summertime Carnival

This is typical of many local fairs and carnivals often
organized by volunteer firemen.

Clearfield County Fair

Sponsored by the Clearfield Volunteer Fire Department.
The first Clearfield County fair was held in 1860.

Tattoo Booth

Clearfield County Fair.

Circus

Traveling circuses still play in smaller rural towns where sometimes the whole town turns out for the occasion.
This one, Walker Bros., which winters in Sarasota, Florida, starts out in the spring working through
the Carolinas, into Virginia, on to Pennsylvania, and then west to Ohio, Michigan,
and the Midwest states before returning south in late fall.
Comprised of clown, juggling, animal, acrobatic, trampoline and trapeze acts, this circus
operates around the nucleus of five families which have been circus performers for many years.
Moving from town to town, they usually perform twice daily, often seven days a week,
spending only one or two days in a town.

Patchinville Barn

Located along Route 219,
this barn burned shortly after this picture was taken.
Of interest are the louvers,
which provide cross-ventilation.

Farmhouse

Knobsville Barn

Mountain Laurel

This evergreen shrub, the state flower of Pennsylvania,
blooms in late June with rose-colored and white flowers.
It is often abundant in mountain woodlands,
frequently along rural roads.

Indian Pipe

This small four-to-six-inch leafless flower
blooms mid to late June on the forest floor,
often in deep leaf mold.

Unfolding of Springtime Ferns
on the Forest Floor

Butterfly and Goldenrod

Garden Spider

A black and yellow Argiope spider.

Shapiro Movie Theater

Located in Mt. Union, this theater was
built in 1915, closed in 1970, and demolished in 1997.

Volunteer Fire Department

Port Matilda.
Volunteer fire departments often sponsor
community fund-raising events and
serve as centers of social activity.

County Fair Farm Exhibit

Centre Hall Grange Encampment and Fair

Centre County.
The Grange Fair, first held in 1874, is the last old-time tenting fair in the country.
Attended by nearly 2,300 families and comprised of over 950 military-style tents,
with many others in campers and motor homes, the event has seen as many as five
generations of the same family return year after year to the same camping spot.
With grandstand acts, midway attractions, horticulture displays,
livestock judging, auctions, and farm exhibits of all types,
the week's festivities are attended by as many as 140,000 persons.

Vehicle Parking at Grange Fair

Grange Fair Tenting

Gospel Tent Crusade and Revival

Along Route 322.

Mahaffey Camp Meeting and Bible Conference

Route 879, Clearfield County.
One of the few religious camp meeting conference sites remaining.
Established in 1894 by the Christian Missionary and Alliance Church.

Pine Forest and Ferns

These trees were planted in 1933
by the U.S. Civilian Conservation Corps.
(following pages)

Campgrounds

Backyard Mushrooms

Hungry Birds

Gillingham Methodist Church

Built in 1897. The church services date to 1838.

Eden Church

Near Shawville.

Presbyterian Church

Route 522, Main Street, Shirleysburg.
Erected in 1830.

Boardman Church

This church was moved to this location
from the ghost town of Gazzam in 1910.
(facing page)

Barn Door Latch

Ducks on an Amish Farm

Early Barn Construction

Mail Pouch and Kentucky Club Barn

Junction of Routes 969 and 219.

School Bus Stop

Demolished in 1997.

Tusseyville Emmanuel Union Church

Built in 1837; rebuilt in 1879.

John Patton, Jr., 1783-1848
Susan Antes Patton, 1791-1883

Curwensville Oak Hill Cemetery

William Irvin, Jr., 1801-1869
Jane Patton Irvin, 1812-1881

Huntingdon Riverview Cemetery

John Patton, 1745-1804
Jane Bartholomew Davis Patton, 1752-1832
In 1776, John Patton was a major in the 1st Battalion of a regiment of
Pennsylvania Riflemen organized to defend the city of Philadelphia.
In 1777, he was appointed by General George Washington to the position of colonel
in command of one of sixteen new regiments authorized by the Continental Congress.
Considered a friend of Washington's, in 1778 he was appointed to Washington's
personal guard, called the Commander-in-Chief's Guard.
In 1779, he was elected to the First Troop, Philadelphia City Cavalry.
After his arrival in Centre County, he and Samuel Miles established an iron furnace
along the Benner Pike in State College.
He was buried with his sword and scabbard.
Family history has it that Washington was godfather at the christening of Patton's son,
John Patton, Jr., who later settled in Curwensville.

Goshen Church Cemetery

Hillcrest Cemetery in Autumn Mist
(following pages)

Ansonville Fruit Hill Church

One of the early "circuit riding" churches of Rev. Frederick Gregory Betts of Clearfield,
the first church was built here in 1841.
Rev. Betts gave the only monetary contribution, fifteen dollars, toward its construction.
Other donations of labor and materials were given by the congregation.
Prior to this time, Rev. Betts preached any day of the week
in homes, barns, schools, or other buildings.
The present church was built in 1878.

Patchinville Cemetery

John Patchin and wife Elizabeth.
Known as "The Spar King," John was the first of the early lumbermen
on the West Branch of the Susquehanna River to provide many of the
white pine spars for the masts of the great sailing ships of the time.
Spars for clippers and "tall" ships were as long as
ninety to one hundred feet of straight unblemished white pine.
Patchin died on December 31, 1863.

Leitzinger's Dept. Store

234 East Market Street.
Established 1882; closed 1996.
Official name was Leitzinger Bros.

Shaw Bros. Grocery

101 West Nichols Street.

Workmans Grocery Store

221 West Nichols Street.

Clearfield Furs

Established 1915; closed 1990.

O. U. A. M.

11 West Nichols Street.
Clearfield Council, Order of
United American Mechanics No. 281.

1901

1920

1954

1964

1994

Kurtz Bros.

A Clearfield-based century-old school supply and equipment and printing enterprise,
led to enduring success by four generations of the Kurtz family.
Kurtz Bros. has been guided by one slogan:
"Our Word Is Our Bond"
and one aim:
*"To follow sound ethical principles in the conduct of our business,
and to put every transaction on the highest plane of business honor."*

Robby

Enjoying the family tradition of cutting
his own Christmas tree, at age five.

Sammy

Smelling the flowers, at age one.

Backyard Pond with Rhododendrons

Afterword

Rob & Marilyn in the Backyard

Unlike a painting, a photograph must deal with what is present. Buildings, roads, trees, the sky, telephone poles and wires can't be moved, only the photographer and the camera can move. If it's an overcast day and you want white puffy clouds, you're just plain out of luck. Yes, I know that technology can and increasingly will change these conditions, but I seek the reality of photographing scenes and animals as they are.

No sky or cloud formation will ever be quite the same again. Light is ever-changing. If a picture of a certain plant or event is missed, sometimes up to a year must pass before the opportunity presents itself again. An outdoor photographer is always aware of the weather and its changes. A dry summer or a wet winter can change everything. Some pictures are gone in a moment, perhaps never to be captured again.

These photographs are what I have seen and recorded with my camera. No props were used: no filters, no extra lighting, and almost never a tripod. The equipment is a 35mm hand-held SLR camera and a few lenses. This may not make for pictures as perfect as others could take, but I try to photograph as nearly as the eye sees. To me, the art is in the composition. Often an incredible amount of film has been used just to get that one good picture at just the right angle, with the right composition in the right light. Sometimes you never get just what you envision.

As I consider the composition of a photograph, I try to be aware of my own experience and emotions. In this sense, all photographs come from within. In photography, it is important to see what is unnoticed by others.

I have often photographed buildings, not for their architectural value alone, but to capture some of the atmosphere left by the people who passed that way. Upon seeing abandoned buildings, I find myself wondering not only about the craftsmen who designed and built them, but about who lived there—their joys, sorrows, successes, and failures. How many joyous Christmas mornings, birthdays, happy days, days of love and wonder, even days of sorrow and death did they experience? Who were these people, and what were their lives? These questions are intriguing; their answers provide a view of history. We know places and buildings by who or what person or family lived in a particular house or building, or by who walked upon that particular ground.

This book has been compiled for your enjoyment, but even more than that, I hope to have created a useful historical and pictorial document for the future. If those who read and look at it decades from now value and enjoy it, then it will have served its purpose.

We all move on, we all change, new people and institutions come to take the place of the old and the present, yet all build upon what has gone before. Sinclair Lewis well expressed this when he wrote in the preface to *Main Street*, "That this Ford car might stand in front of the Bon Ton store, Hannibal invaded Rome and Erasmus wrote in Oxford cloisters."

Without the past, the present could not be. A different past means a different present. In this book I have sought to capture and preserve aspects of the present so that, in the future, others can look at some of the elements of Americana that have molded their own environment.

Meyers Science Notebook

This notebook, compiled in 1823 by Henry Meyers of Hanover, Pa.,
is of interest because of his lists of early science experiments.
Among them are how to make Rice Flour Glue, how to Cast Figures in
Imitation of Ivory, how to Preserve Sheepskins, and how to Case Harden Iron, to
the Method of Making Transparent Soap, the Modes of Whitening Straw,
and The Hour of Day or Night Told by a Suspended Shilling.
Much other data used in that era is included.

Historical Notes

A number of cemeteries, buildings, and other photographs in this book relate to Robert (Robby) Marsh Kurtz, Colin Kurtz Earl, and Garrett William Kurtz as grandchildren of the following:

Great-Great-Great-Great-Great-Great-Grandparents
William (1765-1847) and Elizabeth Anderson (1768-1857) Ewing (parents of Mary Ewing)
Benjamin (1733-1822) and Abigail Lockwood (1738-?) Betts, Jr. (parents of Ebenezer Betts)
John (1745-1804) and Jane Bartholomew Davis (1752-1832) Patton (parents of John Patton, Jr.)

Great-Great-Great-Great-Great-Grandparents
John (1785(6)-1824) and Mary Ewing (1790-1871) Murray (parents of Alexander Murray)
John (1783-1848) and Susan Antes (1791-1883) Patton, Jr. (parents of Jane Patton)
Ebenezer (1766-1846) and Sally Gregory (1770-1868) Betts (parents of Rev. Frederick Gregory Betts)

Great-Great-Great-Great-Grandparents
Henry (1796-1881) and Catherine Winebrenner (1798-1875) Meyers (parents of Eliza Ann Meyers)
Alexander (1812-1889) and Isabella Meek Holt (1820-1879) Murray (parents of Thomas Holt Murray).
Married February 23, 1843, by Rev. F. G. Betts below.
William (1801-1869) and Jane Patton (1812-1881) Irvin, Jr. (parents of Margaret Johnston Irvin)
Rev. Frederick Gregory (1812-1845) and Cornelia Finley (1814-1853) Betts
(parents of William Wilson Betts)

Great-Great-Great-Grandparents
John Christian Julius (1835-1915) and Eliza Ann Meyers (1836-1919) Kurtz
(parents of Charles Theodore Kurtz)
Thomas Holt (1845-1916) and Jennie Reighard (1847-1907) Murray
(parents of Isabella Holt Murray)
William Wilson (1838-1896) and Margaret Johnston Irvin (1839-1910) Betts
(parents of William Irvin Betts)

Great-Great-Grandparents
Charles Theodore (1874-1956) and Pauline Stutz (1875-1964) Kurtz
(parents of Robert Meyers Kurtz, Sr., 1903-1988)
William Irvin (1870-1946) and Isabella Holt Murray (1875-1939) Betts
(parents of Dorothy Betts Kurtz, 1907-1989)

Acknowledgments

McLaughin Photography / Clearfield Camera Center
Clearfield, Pennsylvania

Sheckler Photographics
State College, Pennsylvania

Dr. Roy Buck and Pat Little for their advice
on photographic content.

William I. Betts, III for reviewing the manuscript.

And, of course, Murphy Communications.

And finally, my parents, Robert M. and Dorothy (Betts) Kurtz
who gave me a deep appreciation and interest in
history, literature and especially family.

About This Book

This book was composed in Adobe PageMaker 6.5 for Windows 95.
The typefaces used are, on the cover; Carpenter, Stone Serif, and Stone Serif Bold
in the main body of the book; Nuance and Garamond No. 4 Condensed.

The pages are printed on 110# Reflections by Consolidated,
chosen for its weight, glossy finish, and brilliant white color.

The design, layout, and production of this book was done by
Murphy Communications, State College, Pennsylvania.
The images were scanned and color corrected to match the original
photographs by SFC Graphics, Toledo, Ohio.
The printing was by Jostens Commercial Printing and Publishing,
State College, Pennsylvania